A note for parents

At Fun Learning Resources we design resources that explore love, because people learn best when they are inspired.

The activities in this pack have been chosen to encourage children to explore, research and to get creative. Many of the activities can be completed independently but support should be given as is appropriate for your child. QR codes are for your convenience but do check suitability before use.

If you enjoy this resource then please take a look at our other themes at funlearningresources.com. Thank you for supporting our small family run business.

Download your free logbook and keep a record of the themes you've completed.

Cut the circle from the back of the book.

Tag us in your pictures:

FUN.LEARNING_RESOURCES

funlearningresources.com

Your Learning Journey

This journal is designed to guide your learning as you explore Halloween. To get the most out of it, you'll need a few books, interesting websites and some planned field trips.

List some questions you have.

List some things you want to watch.

Fieldtrip ideas...

Choose some books about Halloween.

HALLOWEEN

MY SPOOKY OUTFIT

FAVOURITES

TREAT:
chocolate digestives

COSTUME:
beetlejuice

SCARY MOVIE:
_____

MY NAME IN CREEPY LETTERS:

CLAUDIA

FAVOURITE THING ABOUT HALLOWEEN:

it's the one day everyone dresses like me.

HAPPY HALLOWEEN

Secret Code

Use the secret code below to figure out the message.

A	B	C	D	E	F	G	H	I	J	K	L	M

N	O	P	Q	R	S	T	U	V	W	X	Y	Z

LET'S HAVE SOME

HALLOWEEN FUN!

Halloween House

Add some spooky decorations to the outside of this house.

Bat Facts

Find out some fascinating facts about bats.

Bat Decorations

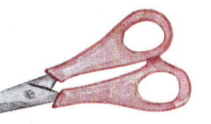

Cut some bat shapes out of black card and use them to decorate your walls (bluetack works well to fix them in place).

Halloween Charades

Cut out these cards to create your own fun game to play with family and friends. Take turns to choose a card and use your acting skills to help players guess what's written on your card.

witch	cauldron
vampire	trick or treat
spider	potion
werewolf	pumpkin

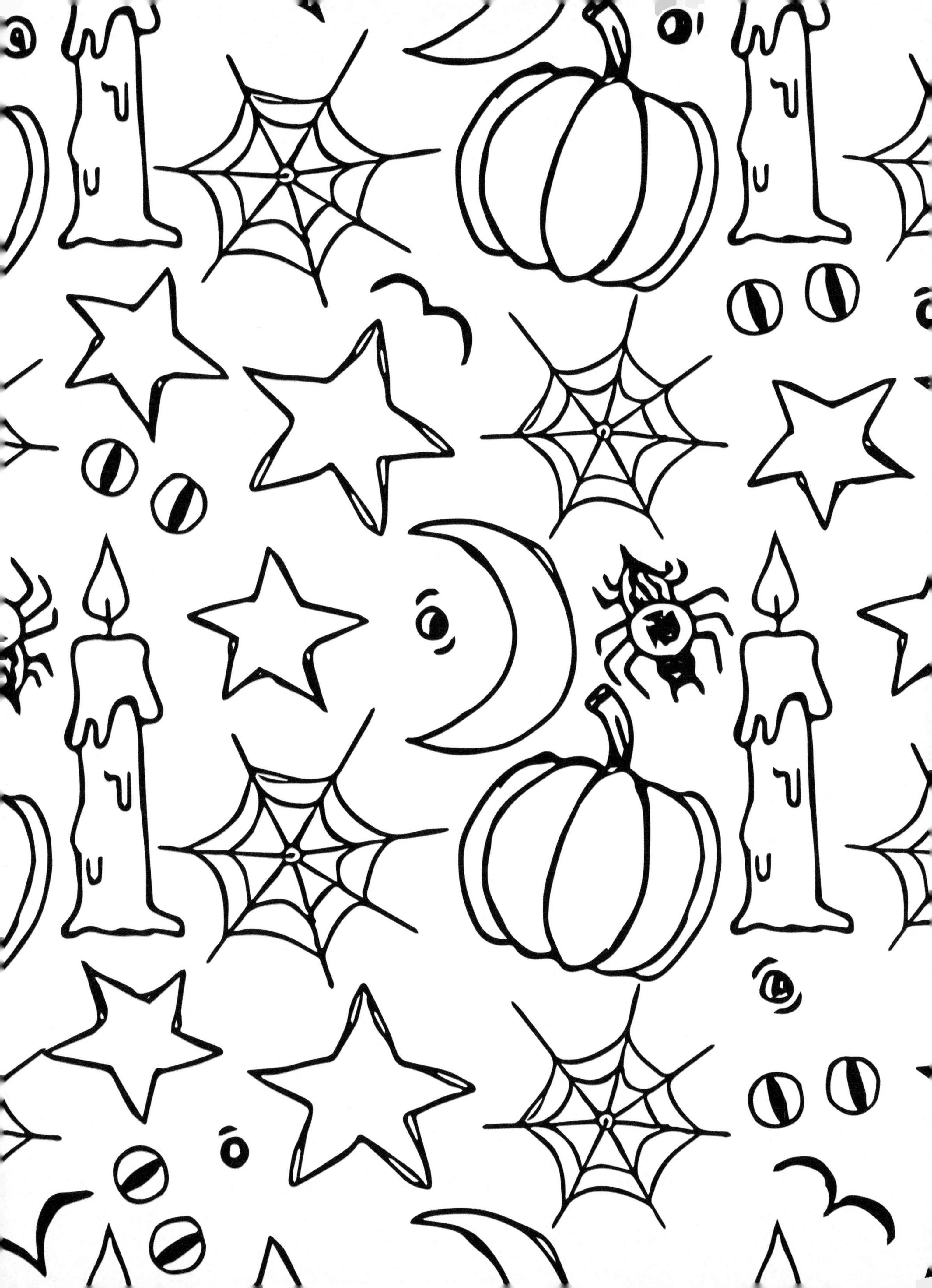

Spiders of Britain

cellar spider

spotted wolf spider

garden spider

rabbit hutch spider

giant house spider

nursery web spider

zebra spider

ladybird spider

raft spider

flower crab spider

wasp spider

Spider Hunt

There are more than 45,000 known species of spider, 650 of those can be found in the UK. How many can you find?

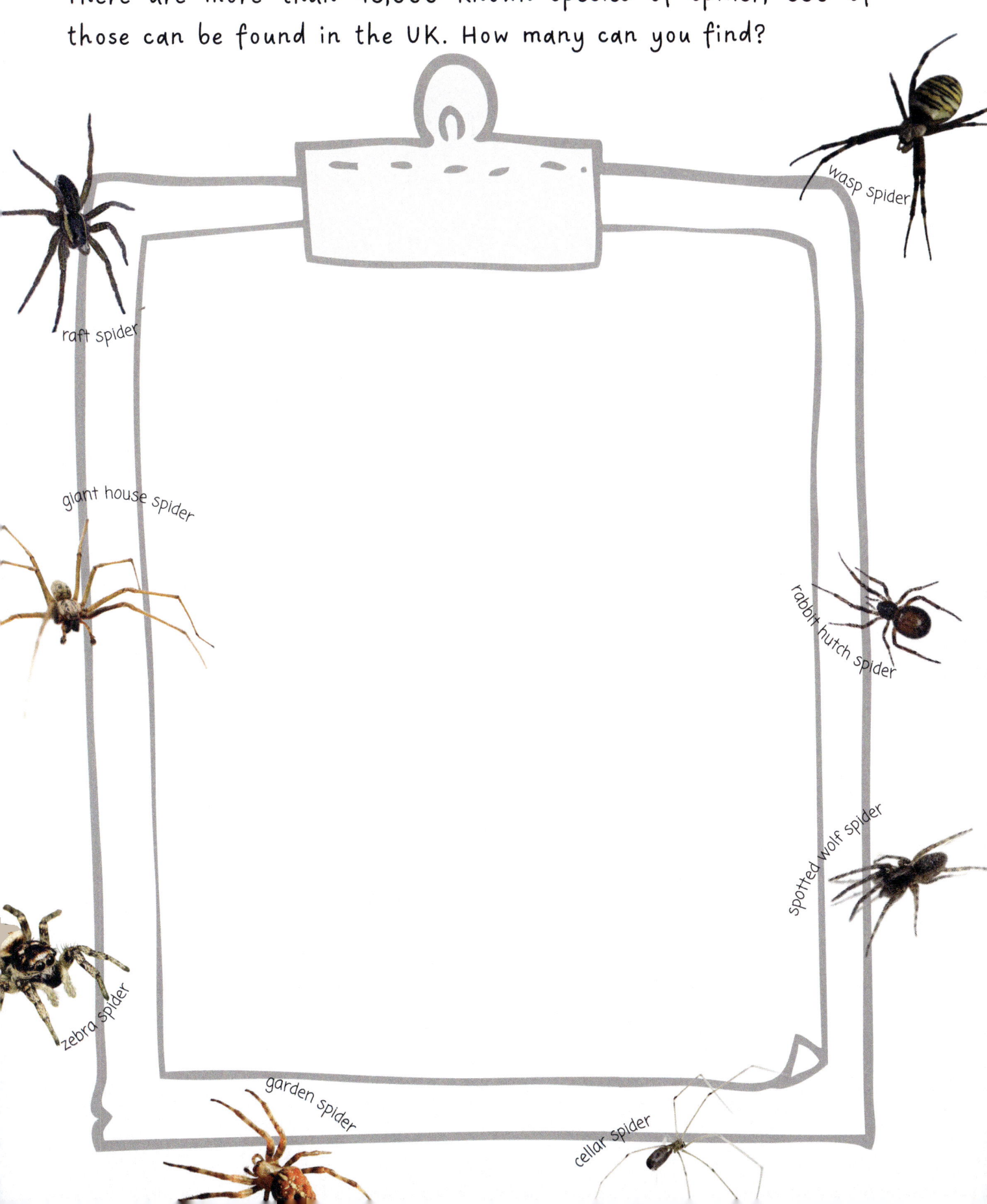

ladybird spider

wasp spider

raft spider

giant house spider

rabbit hutch spider

spotted wolf spider

zebra spider

garden spider

cellar spider

Find Out!

Spider silk is one of the strongest materials on earth! Let's test some materials to see how strong they are.

You will need:

- 3 different cords e.g. dental floss, fishing line, cotton etc
- A hanger
- A pair of scissors
- Pebbles
- A black marker

Directions:

1. Choose a cord and use it to make a web around the coat hanger.
2. Draw some spiders on the pebbles.
3. Carefully place pebbles on your web to see if they will hold.
4. Repeat with your other cords.

What do you notice happening to your web?

Which cord is strongest?

Science Investigation

Prediction:

| Material: | Material: | Material: |

Observations:

Samhain

Halloween originated from ancient Celtic festivals, particularly the festival called Samhain (pronounced sah-win).

Long, long ago, people believed that on the night of October the 31st, the boundary between the living and the spirit world became blurred. They believed that ghosts, witches and other supernatural beings came out and roamed the Earth.

People dressed up in constumes to confuse the spirits and frighten them away. They also lit bonfires and gathered to tell stories, play games and honour their dead.

How will you celebrate Samhain? There are some ideas on the next page.

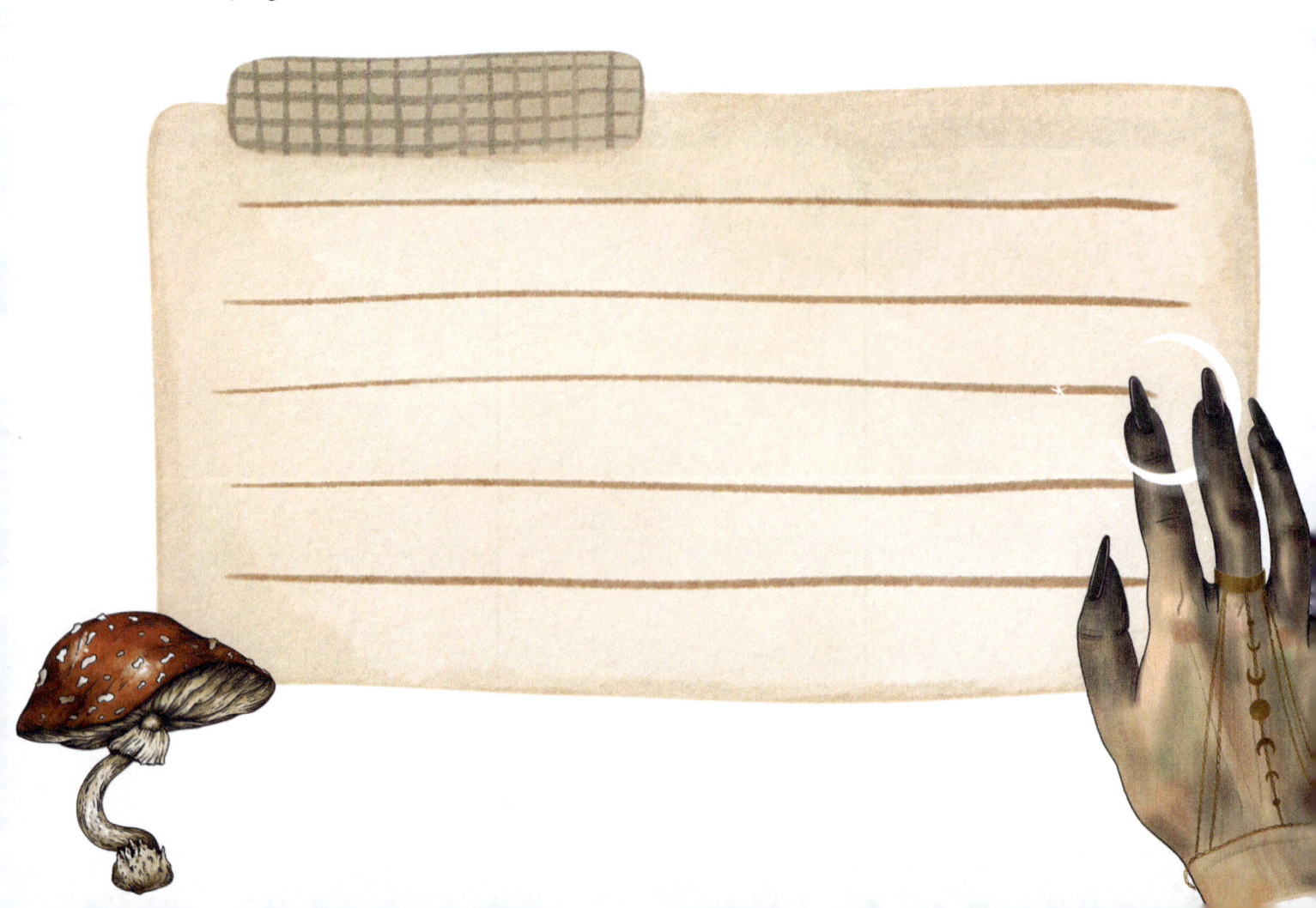

Samhain Activity Ideas

Here are some fun ideas for kids to celebrate Samhain:

- Take a nature walk and collect some autumn leaves to create a nature-inspired centerpiece for your table.

- Dim the lights and gather around to tell stories.

- Create a small altar to honour and remember your ancestors. Ask for help to place photographs, mementos or symbols representing loved ones who have passed away.

- Use seasonal produce to make a meal and talk about the significance of the harvest season.

- Masks have long been associated with Samhain, representing the thinning of the veils between worlds. Get creative with paper plates, paints, markers, feathers, and ribbons and create your own mask.

Cheesy Broomsticks

These edible broomsticks are easy to make and look great!

Rating: ☆☆☆☆☆

You will need:
- pretzel sticks
- cheese strings
- herbs to garnish

Directions:

1. Cut a cheese string in half and carefully peel them about two-thirds the way up.

2. Stick a pretzel-stick inside.

3. Tie each one with a piece of chive or other herb to finish.

Yummy Mummies

These tasty treats are perfect for serving at a Halloween party or movie night.

Rating: ☆☆☆☆☆

You will need:
- ready roll puff pastry
- hotdogs sausages
- icing (for eyes)

Directions:

1. Open your hotdog packet and cut in half to make them shorter.
2. Cut strips of pastry and wrap around each sausage.
3. Bake on 190°C for 15 minutes or until golden brown.
4. Make the eyes using a dot of mustard, ketchup or a poppy seed.

Creepy Comic

Create a creepy comic strip. What characters will you come up with?

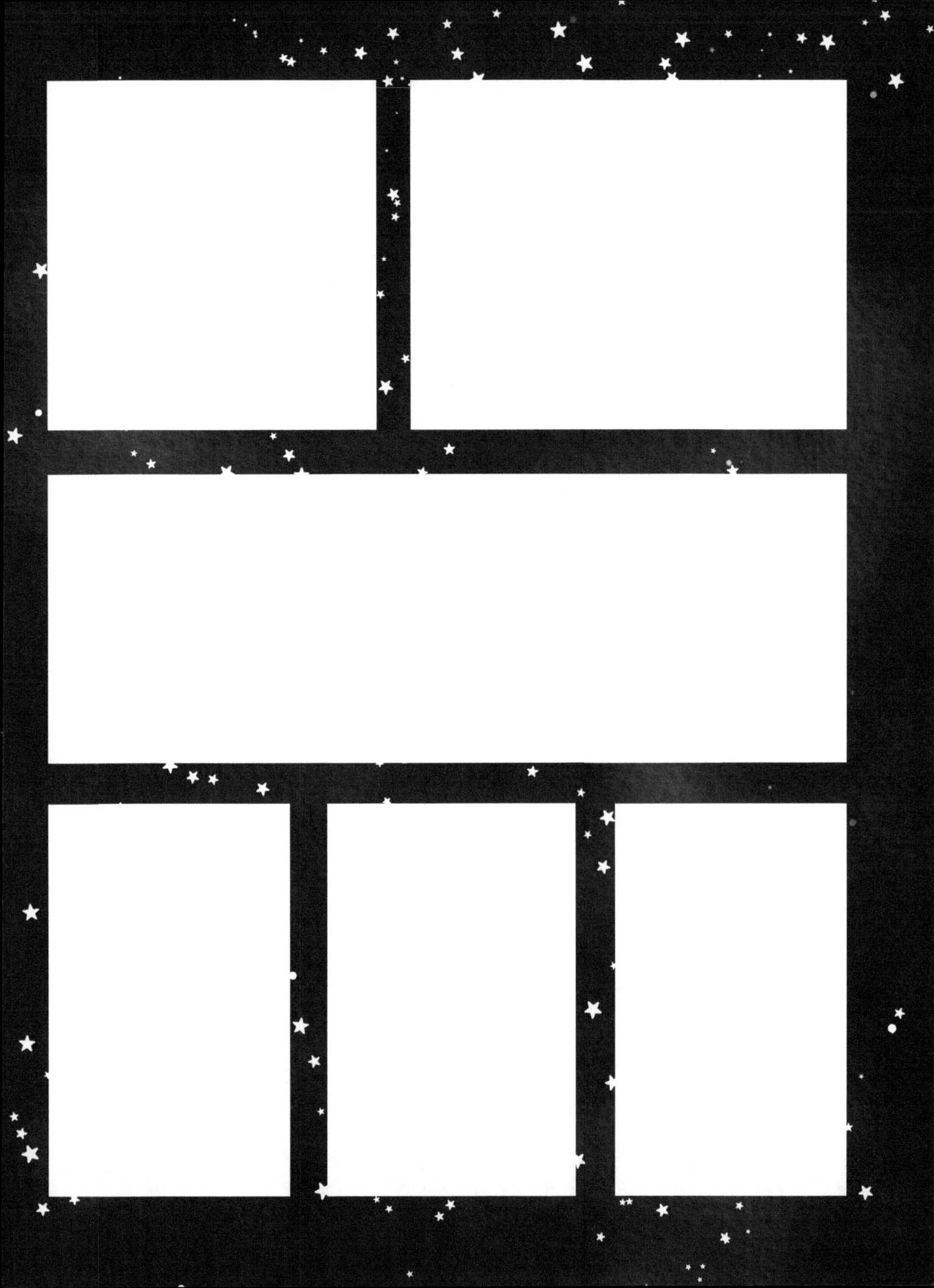

Spooky Eye Spy

I spy with my little eye, something beginning with "g"...

Movie Time

Watch a documentary or film. Will you choose a spooky one?

Title:

Rating:

Spooky Storytelling

Look at this creepy picture and feel inspired...

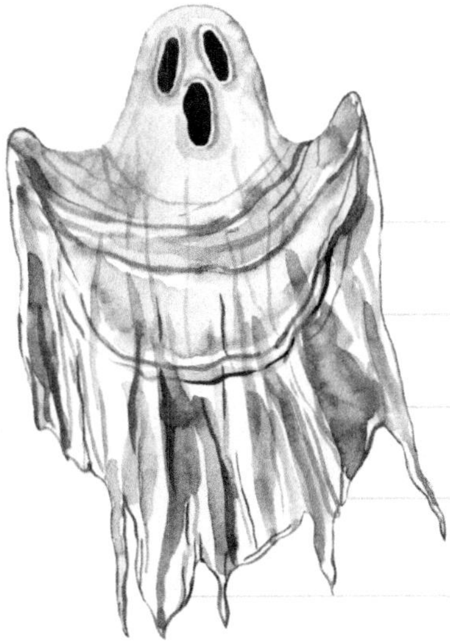

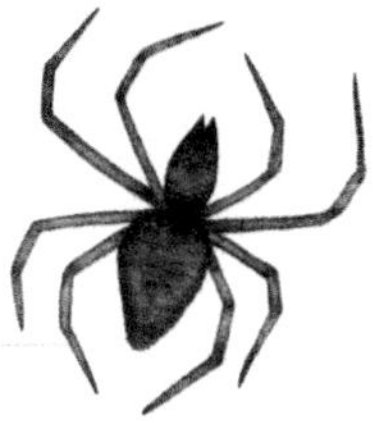

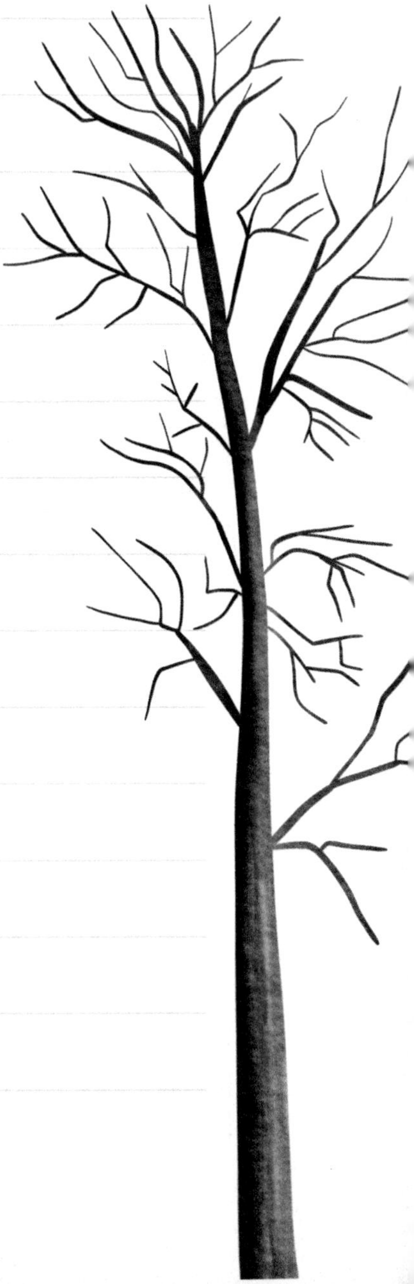

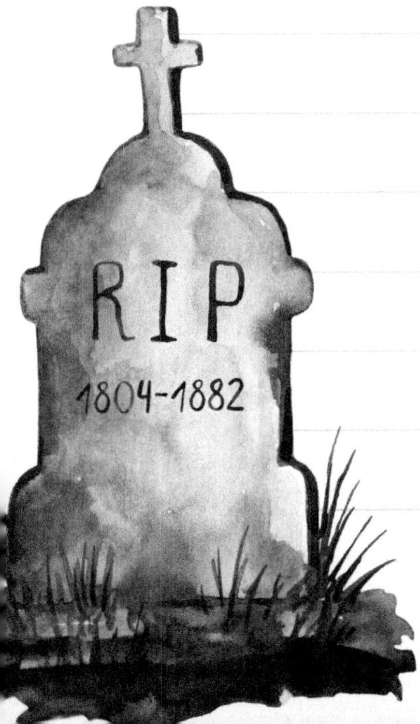
RIP
1804-1882

Spooky Sites

Look at these spooky sites around the world.

Hoia-Baciu Forest, Romania
Some believe this eerie forest is a portal that causes visitors to disappear.

Chuuk Lagoon, Micronesia
In 1944, over 250 aircraft and 50 ships were destroyed and sunk here during WW2.

Catacombs of Paris, France
Buried below the streets of Paris, the Catacombs house the bones of over 6 million people.

Alcatraz, California
In its heyday, this was the ultimate maximum security prison located on a lonely island.

Spooky Sites

Can you find out about or create your own spooky site?

Beastly Burgers

You can fill these burger rolls with your favourite fillings.

Rating: ☆☆☆☆☆

You will need:
- burger buns

Fillings:
- eyes: cucumber, olives, tomatoes, gherkins, onion etc.
- mouth: tomatoes, pepperoni, ketchup, sausages, burger etc.
- teeth: onions, cheese etc.
- cocktail sticks for fixing in place

Directions:
1. Fill your burger buns.
2. Use cocktail sticks to fix eyes in place.
3. Serve with a scowl!

Freaky Fruit

Grab your favourite fruits and make them freaky! You could use icing, chocolate or strawberry sauce, mini marshmallows and edible eyes.

Rating: ☆☆☆☆☆

Pumpkin Pizza

The perfect pizza for an autumn feast.

Rating: ☆☆☆☆☆

You will need:

Dough:
- 500g strong flour
- 1 tsp salt
- 1 tsp yeast
- 300ml warm water
- oil, for greasing

Tomato sauce:
- tomato passata
- sprinkle of sugar
- garlic

Topping:
- pepperoni
- grated cheese

Directions:

1. Mix the dry dough ingredients in a bowl and add the water gradually to form a dough.
2. Knead the dough for 5 minutes and leave in a warm place.
3. Roll dough into a pumpkin shape.
4. Combine the tomato sauce ingredients and spread on top.
5. Decorate the top with toppings and cook for 15 minutes until golden.

Halloween Costume

Design a Halloween costume.

Terrifying Tales

The moon hung in the darkened sky, casting an eerie glow over the desolate town. The wind whispered through the trees, carrying with it an unsettling chill. Shadows danced and twisted along the dimly lit streets, concealing secrets that would send a shiver down anyone's spine.

It was on this ominous night that young Emily found herself walking alone, her footsteps echoing eerily against the cobblestone. Little did she know that her path would lead her to a long abandoned house, its broken windows and crumbling facade beckoning her closer...

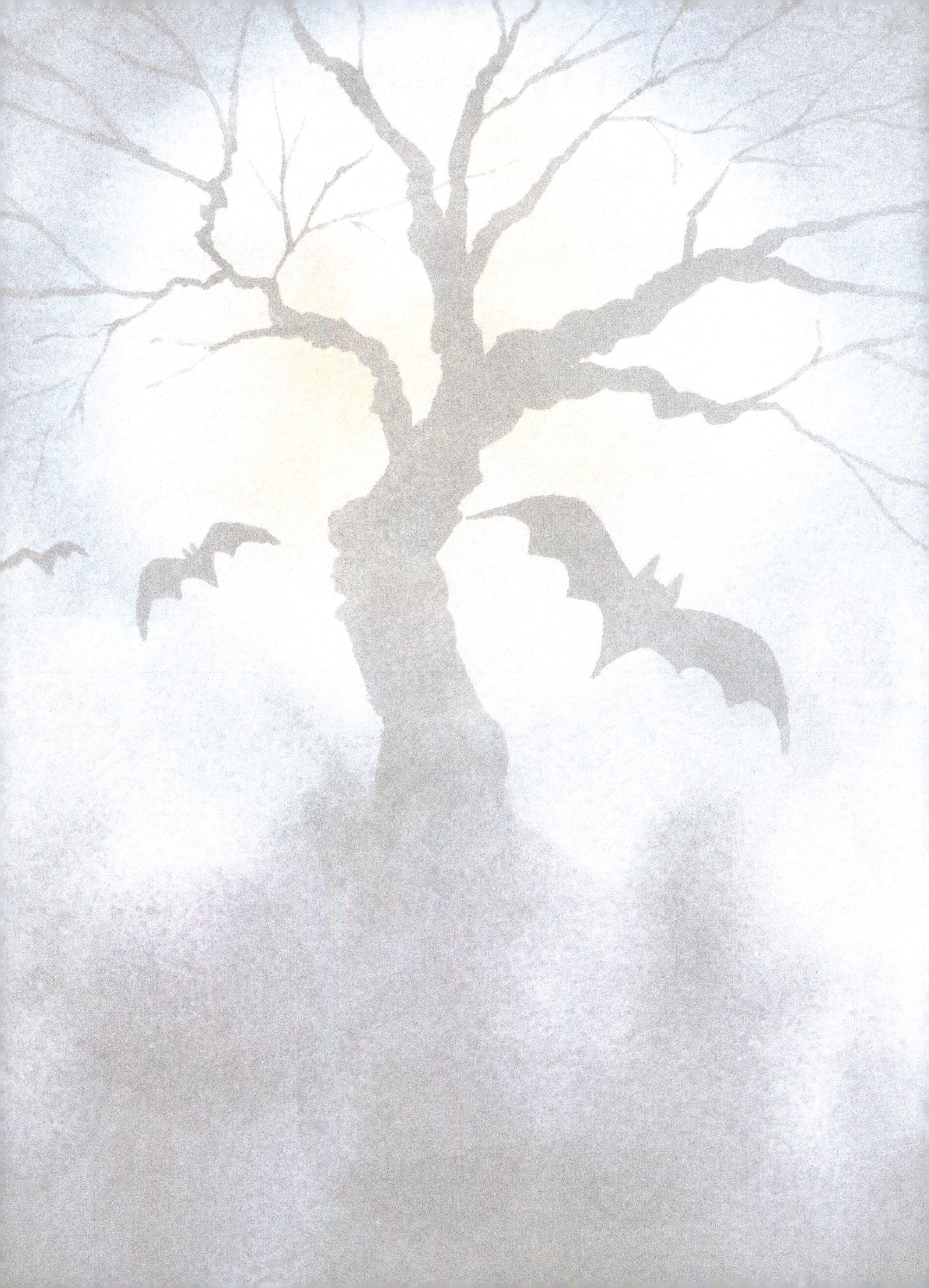

Terrifying Tangerines

These terrifying tangerines make a tasty treat! Simply use a marker to draw on the tangerine peel and display them until you're ready to eat one.

Halloween Scavenger Hunt

- ◯ pumpkin
- ◯ skull
- ◯ black cat
- ◯ witch's hat
- ◯ cauldron
- ◯ eyeball
- ◯ broomstick
- ◯ bat
- ◯ sweets
- ◯ tombstone
- ◯ cobweb

Black Cats

Black cats have long been associated with Halloween. One belief is that they were considered to be companions of witches and were said to possess magical powers. This gave them a bad reputation and they became a symbol of evil. People even thought that witches could transform themselves into black cats to evade capture.

You will need:

- black construction card
- white chalk or crayons

Directions:

- Draw and cut out a silhouette of a cat, emphasizing the shape of the cat's body, ears, and tail.
- Use white chalk or crayons to create a spooky moonlit background or add details like glowing eyes to your cat.
- Glue your cat in place and display your masterpiece.

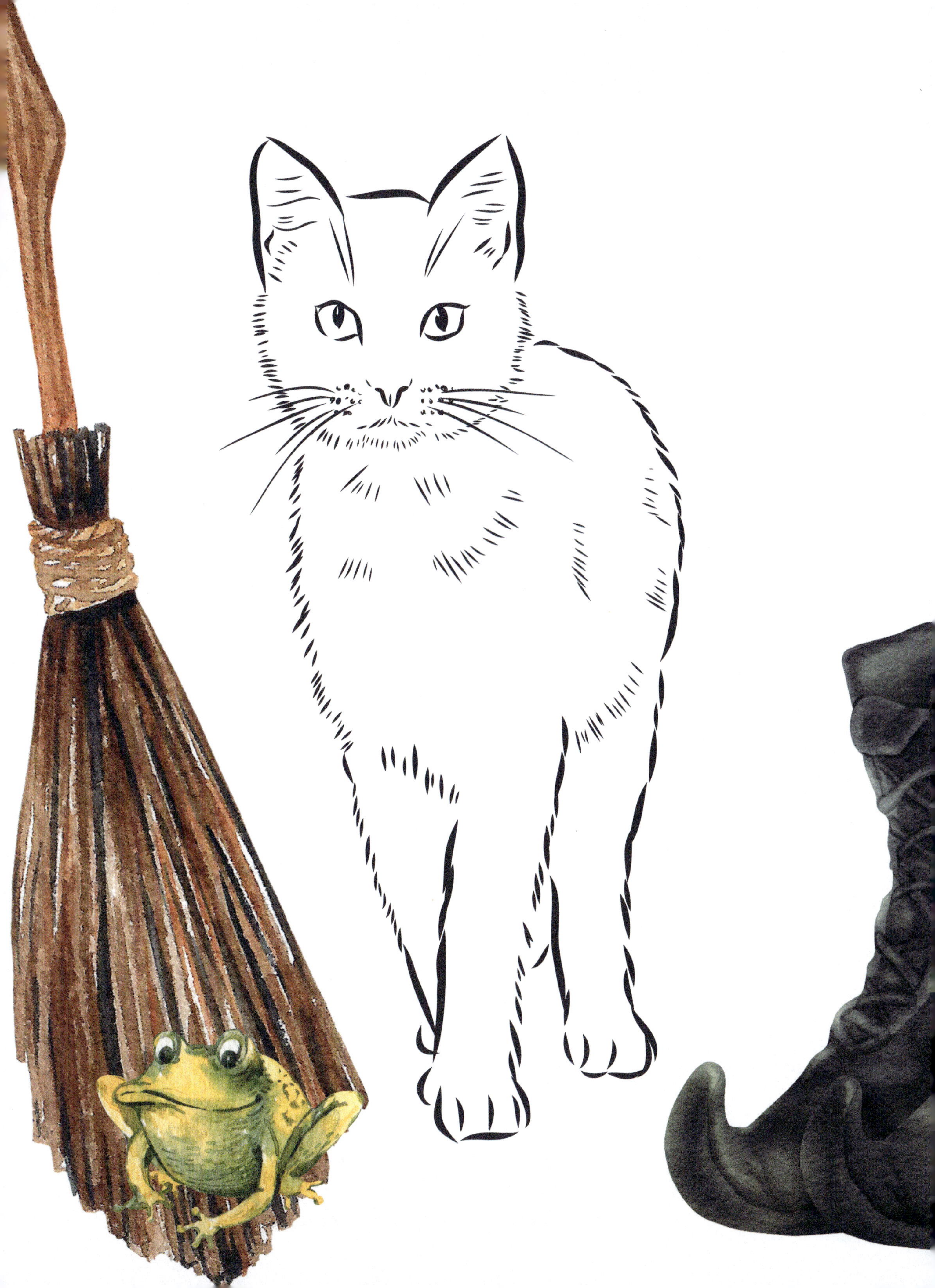

Wonderful Witch's Pet

Every witch needs a pet but it doesn't have to be a black cat. What pet would you have if you were a witch?

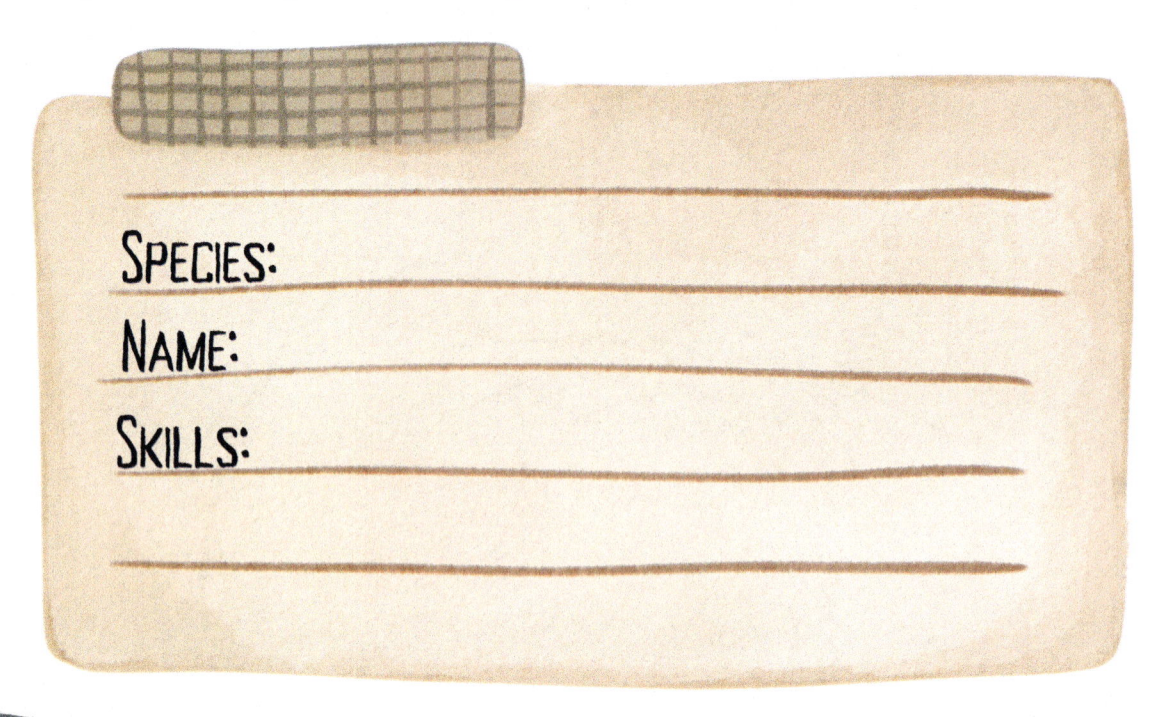

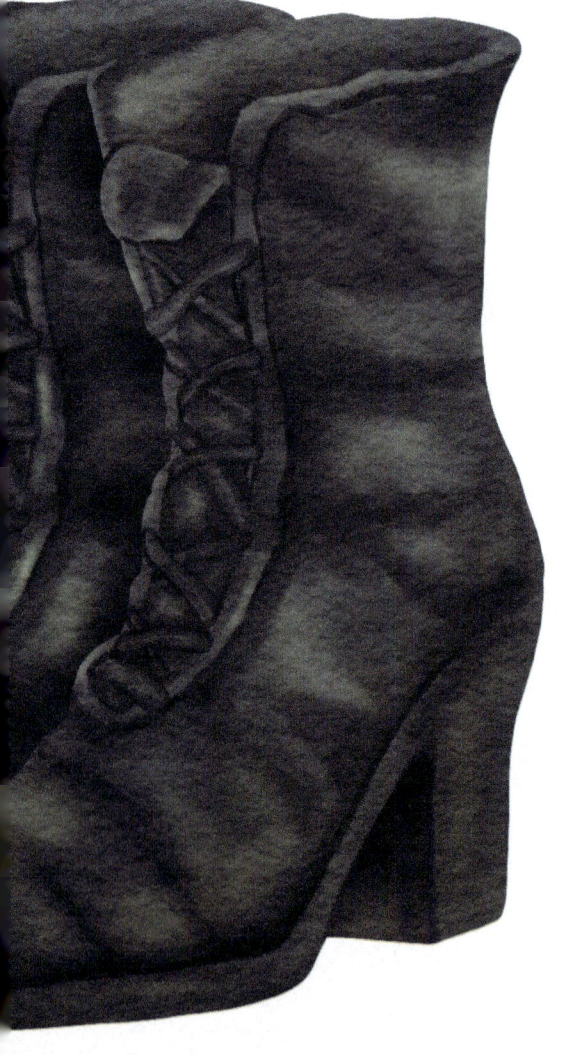

SPECIES:
NAME:
SKILLS:

Help the ghost to find the haunted house.

Decorate This...

The owners of this house need some help to get it ready for Halloween. Add some spooky decorations...you could even draw a skeleton sitting on the chair!

The Ultimate Treat

Design the ultimate Halloween sweet for trick-or-treaters:

INGREDIENTS

IT WILL TASTE:

o————————————o

IT WILL FEEL:

o————————————o

IT WILL SMELL:

o————————————o

THE NAME OF MY SWEET:

A SKELETON HOLDING MY SWEET:

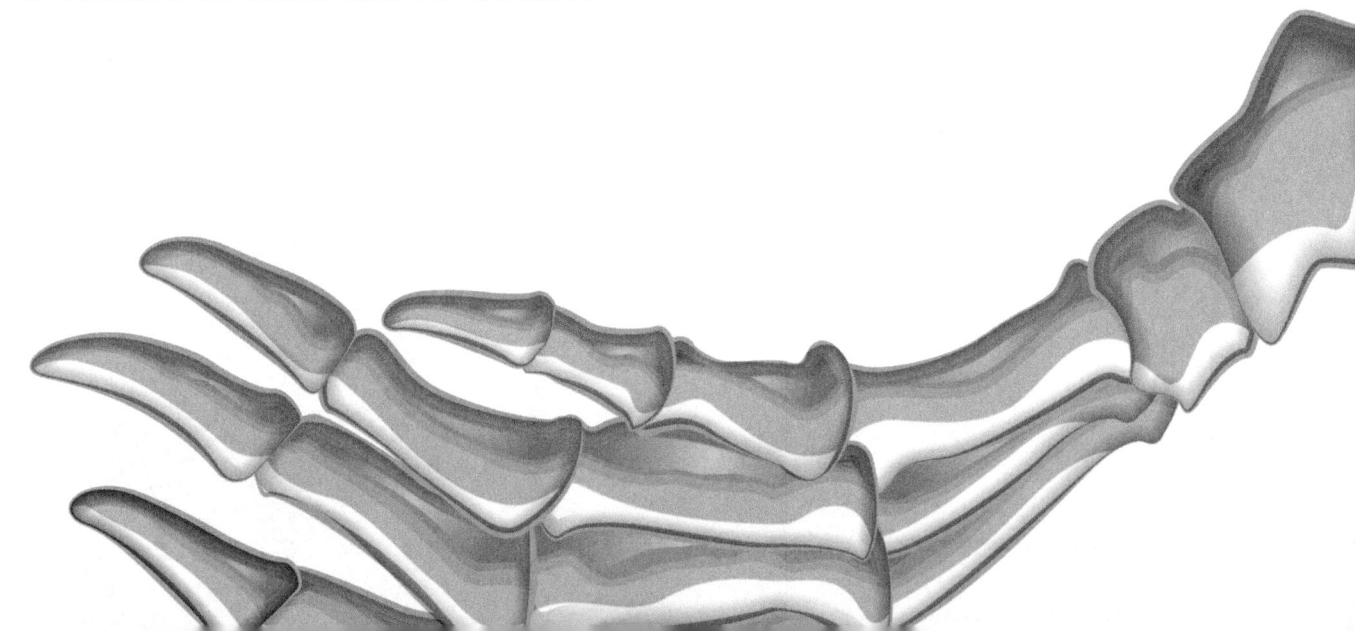

Haunted House

Every haunted house needs something scary haunting it! Get creative and come up with a monster or ghoul for each of these spooky houses.

Bones!

See how many of these bones you can label.

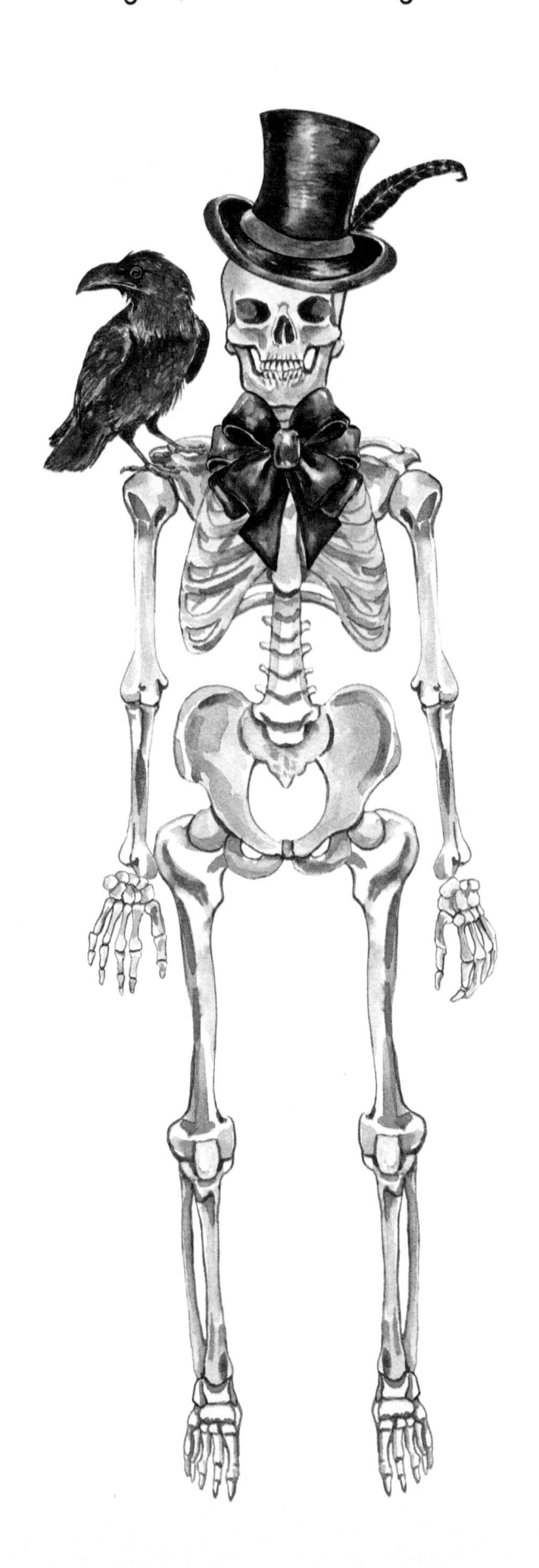

Facepaint Fun

Use crayons to add facepaint designs to these faces.

Creepy Creatures

Add some creepy creatures to this old tree.

Spider Races

You will need:
- Plastic toy spiders (one per player)
- Straws
- Masking tape or string

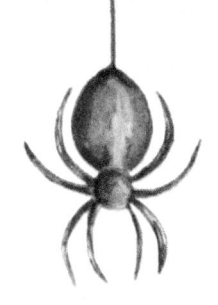

Directions:

1. Set up a race track on a smooth surface by marking a starting line and a finish line using masking tape or string.

2. Give each player a plastic toy spider.

3. Line up the spiders on the starting line.

4. Players use their straws to blow air and move their spiders forward to race to the finish line.

Change it up:
- Race against yourself. Use a stop watch to time yourself.
- Create obstacles or challenges along your race track. Add loops, curves, barriers or tunnels to create the ultimate track.
- Decorate your race track area with Halloween-themed decorations.
- Get players to name their spiders and give them creative backstories e.g. Hairy Legs Harold who ran away from the circus and has been living in the attic ever since.
- Make some small prizes or certificates for the winners of each race or every spider that completes the treacherous track!

Halloween Mad Libs

Fill in the blanks with the corresponding parts of speech (noun, verb, adjective) to create a hilariously spooky story.

Adjectives

Adjectives are words that describe things. They tell us how something looks, feels, or what it's like. They help to make our sentences more interesting and give us more information. For example, "cute" could describe a kitten and "scary" could describe a Halloween costume.

Nouns

Nouns give names to everything around us, like people, places, and objects. They help us talk about and understand the world. A noun is a word like "table", "pumpkin" or "Frankenstein".

Verbs

Verbs are action words that show what someone or something is doing. They make our sentences more lively and help us express what is happening. A verb is a word like "hopping" or "hop", "hiding" or "hide".

Once upon a time, on a (adjective) _____ Halloween night, I went (verb) _____ with my (noun) _____. As we walked down the (noun) _____ we could hear the (adjective) _____ sound of leaves (verb) _____ in the wind.

Suddenly, we came across a (adjective) _____ (noun) _____. It had (number) _____ (noun) _____ glowing in the dark. We cautiously entered and were greeted by a (adjective) _____ (noun) _____.

The (noun) _____ offered us a (adjective) _____ potion. We took a sip and felt (adjective) _____. It gave us the power to (verb) _____ like never before.

We continued our (adjective) _____ adventure through the haunted (noun) _____. We encountered a (adjective) _____ (noun) _____ and a (adjective) _____ (noun) _____.

We laughed and (verb) _____ all night long until the (noun) _____ came up. It was the most (adjective) _____ Halloween night we had ever experienced.

As we (verb) _____ home, we couldn't help but wonder if it was all just a (adjective) _____ dream. But one thing was certain, it was a Halloween we would never (verb) _____!

Monster Muffins

You will need:

- 2 medium eggs
- 125ml vegetable oil
- 250ml semi-skimmed milk
- 250g caster sugar
- 400g self-raising flour
- 1 tsp salt
- 100g chocolate chips (optional)
- Icing pens and sweets for decorating

Directions:

1. Heat the oven to 180°C fan/gas 6.
2. Beat the eggs lightly and add the vegetable oil and milk.
3. Combine the sugar and whisk until you have a smooth batter.
4. Sift in flour and salt and mix until just smooth. Don't over-mix as this will make the muffins tough.)
5. Fill muffin cases with batter and bake for 20-25 mins, until golden.
6. Allow to cool completely before decorating.

Jack-o'-Lanterns

The history of Jack-o'-lanterns dates back to an Irish folktale about a man named Jack. According to legend, Jack invited the Devil to have a drink with him but he didn't want to pay for his drink. He convinced the Devil to turn himself into a coin so that Jack could use him to pay for their drinks.

Once the Devil had transformed into a coin, Jack popped him into his pocket next to a silver cross to stop him from changing back into his original form again.

Eventually Jack freed the Devil, once he agreed that he would not bother Jack and that when the man died he promised that he would not claim his soul.

The story goes that when Jack died, God would not allow him into heaven and the Devil, kept to his word and didn't claim his soul.

Jack was left to wander the Earth carrying only a carved turnip containing a burning coal to light his way.

People began carving their own versions using turnips, beetroots and potatoes and placing a candle inside in an attempt to ward off evil spirits.

When Irish immigrants brought the tradition to America, people began carving pumpkins which were easier to carve and readily available.

Decorate This...

Wicked Witch?

People began accusing anyone they disliked or feared of being witches. Women who lived alone, spent time with animals or practiced "magic" were targeted. What can you find out about witches?

Salem Witch Trials

In 1692 in a town called Salem, Massachusetts a group of young girls started having convulsions that caused them to thrash around uncontrollably. They accused several people of witchcraft.

The town held witch trials to determine whether people were witches or not. These trials were not conducted fairly and many innocent people died.

Over several months, 150 women, men and childen were found guilty of witchcraft and imprisoned or killed.

The trials finally came to an end when someone dared to accuse the wife of the Massachusetts governor. He ordered an end to the arrests and called a stop to the trials,

MARTHA CORY AND HER PERSECUTORS.

Historic Protests

Several people protested (a public expression of objection) against the trials as they believed there were medical reasons for the occurrences of 1692. Design a sign for a protest.

Baba Yaga

Read this description from Slavic mythology before illustrating this strange character. She is portrayed as a witch who flies through the air in a mortar using the pestle to steer. As she flies she sweeps away the tracks using a broom made of silver birch. Her house is a log cabin with giant chicken legs. It's surrounded by a fence made of human bones with skulls on top. The door has a keyhole that's shaped like a mouth filled with vicious teeth.

Potions

Creating your own potions is a great way to make Halloween decorations cheaply or even for free. Gather together some jars, bottles and tubs and fill them with some of these:

- twigs
- fake spiders
- herbs
- ping pong balls painted as eyes
- cotton wool separated to look like cobwebs
- water with food colouring
    - add a drop of oil
    - add a sprinkle of lustre dust
- toy frogs

Label It

Make some labels to add to your bottles. Here are some ideas:

Witch's Brew
Zombie Elixir
Spider Venom
Dried Bat Wing
Ghostly Essence
Werewolf Potion
Potion of Eternal Darkness
Cauldron **C**oncoction
Moonlit **M**agic

Alliteration is a fun literary device to use on your labels. It's when the same letter or sound is used at the beginning of words that are next to each other.

Swamp Slime

- Mix half a cup (120ml) of PVA glue with 2 tablespoons of water.
- Add half a cup of shaving cream and half a tablespoon of bicarbonate of soda.
- Stir in some food colouring.
- Now add around 1 tablespoon of contact lens solution. If it's too sticky add a little more but not too much or it'll loose its stretch.

Remember mixing slime is a chemistry experiment and should be done safely. Wash your hands after use and protect clothes and surfaces.

Double Double toil & trouble
Fire & Burn
CAULDRON BUBBLE

Brewing a Potion

What ingredients would you need to brew a potion that would instantly tidy your room?

INGREDIENTS:

Scary Monsters

People like to dress up as scary monsters for Halloween. Let's find out where the idea of these monsters began...

Werewolves

Werewolves feature in stories from many different cultures around the world. The ancient Greeks have the tale of Lycaon, who was turned into a wolf by Zeus and Norse mythology features tales of berserkers who were fierce warriors said to possess the ability to transform into wolves or bear-like creatures in battle. What would you look like as a werewolf?

The different shapes of the moon that we see at night are called phases. The moon appears different because it orbits around our planet and as it changes position the sun illuminates different parts of its surface. The cycle repeats about every 29.5 days.

Phases Of The Moon

Take a look at the moon tonight? What does it look like?

When do you predict the next full moon will be?

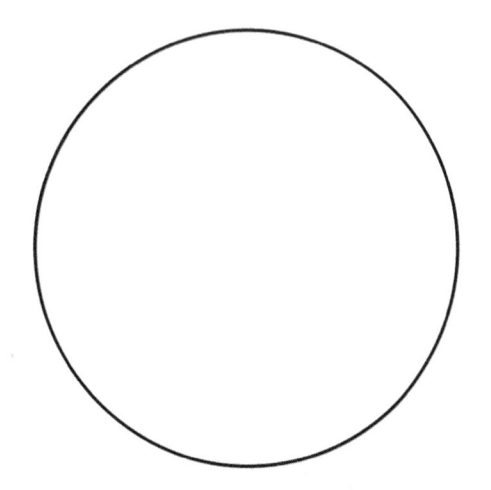

_____

Do some research to find out when the next full moon is due. Was your estimate close?

_____

Waxing crescent | First quarter | Waxing gibbous | Full moon | Waning gibbous | Third quarter | Waning crescent

A Moon Haiku

A haiku is a traditional form of Japanese poetry made up of three lines. The structure of a haiku follows a specific syllable pattern:
- The first line contains five syllables.
- The second line contains seven syllables.
- The third line contains five syllables.

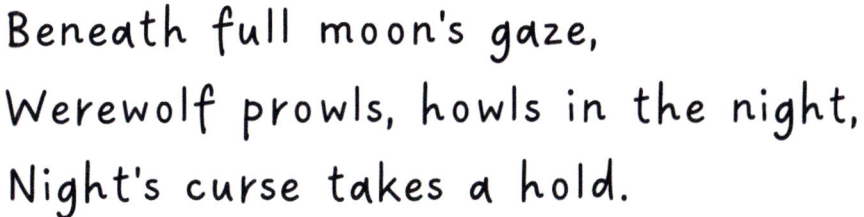

Beneath full moon's gaze,
Werewolf prowls, howls in the night,
Night's curse takes a hold.

Mummies

The ancient Egyptians wrapped the bodies of wealthy people and buried them in hidden tombs with everything they would need for the afterlife. In 1922 when the undisturbed tomb of King Tutankhamun was discovered the idea of "the mummy's curse" spread worldwide. Find out more about the Ancient Egyptians.

> In 1912, a month after the Titanic sank, the Washington Post ran a story suggesting that a mummy's curse was to blame for its demise.

Frankenstein's Monster

Frankenstein's monster, is the main character in Mary Shelley's novel. Mad scientist Victor Frankenstein created a monster using body parts. Collect various images from magazines and arrange and glue the images together to create a Frankenstein-inspired monster collage.

frankenstein

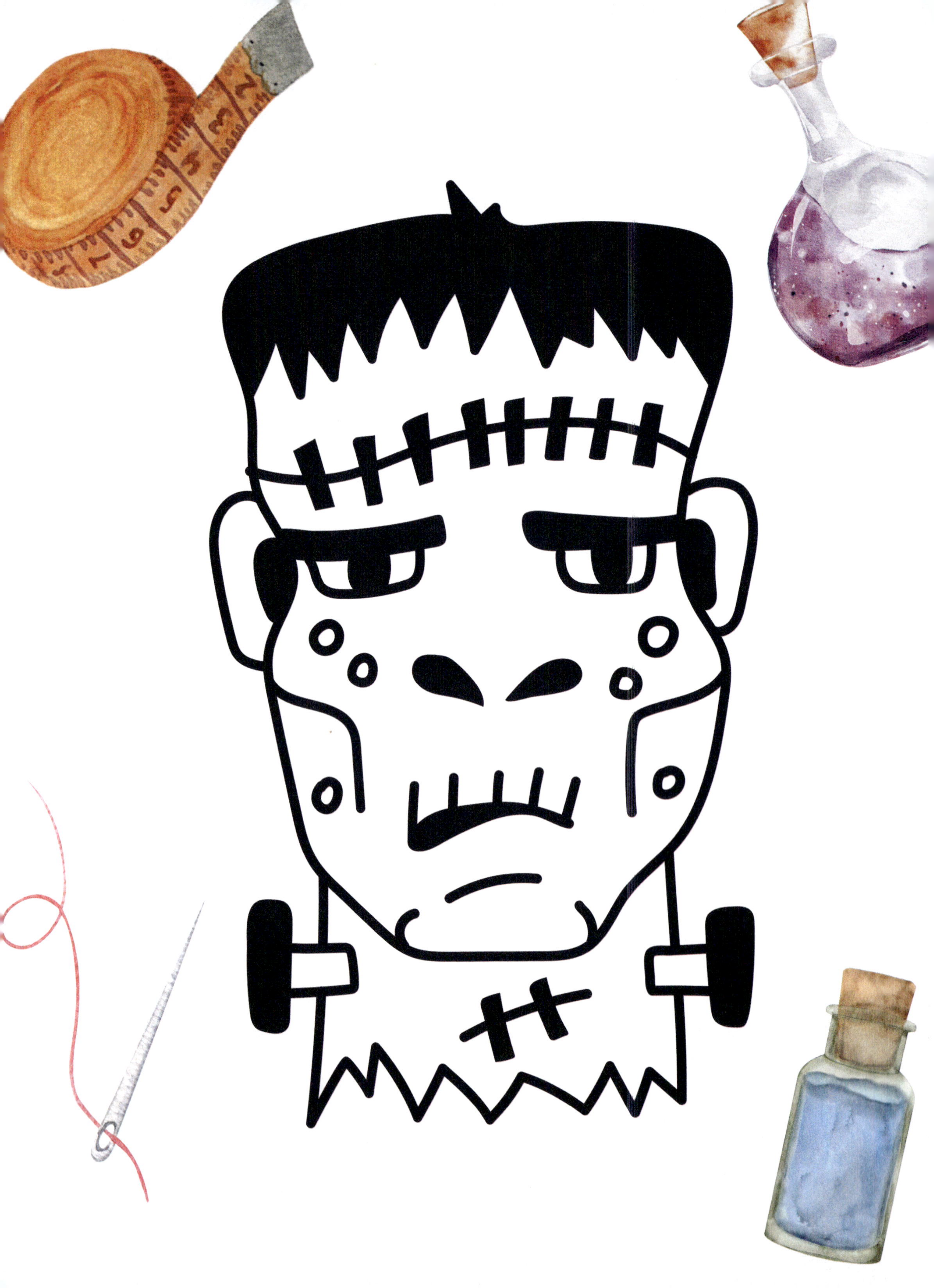

Party Planning

Plan a fun Halloween party for your family or friends.

WHO'S INVITED:

BUDGET:

DECORATIONS:

FOOD:

Design Your Invitations

When you design your invitation you'll need to let people know...

the kind of party you have planned ↓

who's invited ↓

Let's have a Spooktacular time!

Halloween Party

7.00 PM ON HALLOWEEN NIGHT
COSTUMES REQUIRED
SPOOKY HOUSE 131017 STREET
OCTOBER 31ST

To: A SPECIAL GUEST
Address: 217 OFFICE OF
PUMKPIN STREET GHOST 098765

No Tricks - Just Treats

RSVP BY OCTOBER 21ST TO
BLACK CAT AT 120.101.2017

↑ where and when the party is

↑ whether it is fancy dress

↑ when they need to reply by

You'll most likely want your party to be a little scary so use some adjectives like...

spooky   **haunted**   **terrifying**

Spooky Soundtrack

Have a go at making your own scary recording to play at Halloween. Think about what might make creepy sound effects or terrifying background noise.

Brick or Treat

Can you build a tasty treat using bricks or perhaps you can create a spooky monster?

TRICK OR TREAT

More Halloween Activities...

- [ ] Call someone and tell them what you've been learning about.
- [ ] Create a spooky boardgame.
- [ ] Craft your own monster using a sock.
- [ ] Explore an aspect that interested you in more detail.
- [ ] Create an infographic about Halloween.
- [ ] Make an animation (The 'I Can Animate' app is easy to use!)
- [ ] Create some recipes for a spooky feast.
- [ ] Visit a pumpkin farm.
- [ ] Follow a monster drawing tutorial.
- [ ] Make a creepy comic.

OTHER RESOURCES YOU MIGHT LIKE...

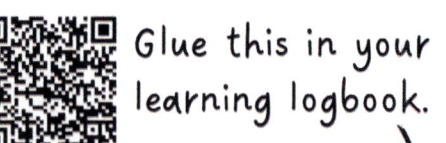

Glue this in your learning logbook.

Printed in Great Britain
by Amazon